play guitar
the jam

down in the tube station at midnight
4

going underground
12

start!
20

strange town
24

the eton rifles
30

town called malice
37

guitar tablature explained
2

translations
44

This publication is not authorised for sale in the United States of America and/or Canada

Wise Publications
London/New York/Paris/Sydney/Copenhagen/Madrid/Tokyo

guitar tablature explained

Guitar music can be notated three different ways: on a musical stave, in tablature, and in rhythm slashes

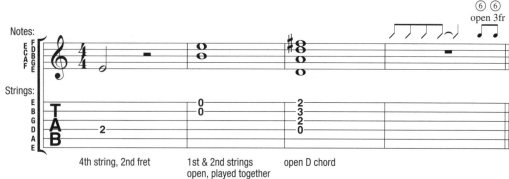

RHYTHM SLASHES are written above the stave. Strum chords in the rhythm indicated. Round noteheads indicate single notes.

THE MUSICAL STAVE shows pitches and rhythms and is divided by lines into bars. Pitches are named after the first seven letters of the alphabet.

TABLATURE graphically represents the guitar fingerboard. Each horizontal line represents a string, and each number represents a fret.

definitions for special guitar notation

SEMI-TONE BEND: Strike the note and bend up a semi-tone (1/2 step).

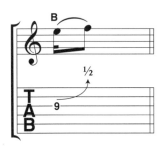

WHOLE-TONE BEND: Strike the note and bend up a whole-tone (whole step).

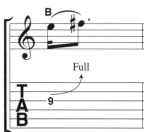

GRACE NOTE BEND: Strike the note and bend as indicated. Play the first note as quickly as possible.

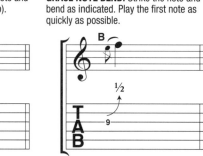

QUARTER-TONE BEND: Strike the note and bend up a 1/4 step.

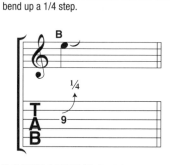

BEND & RELEASE: Strike the note and bend up as indicated, then release back to the original note.

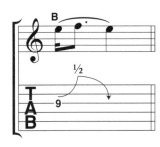

COMPOUND BEND & RELEASE: Strike the note and bend up and down in the rhythm indicated.

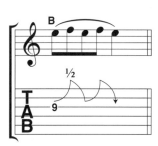

PRE-BEND: Bend the note as indicated, then strike it.

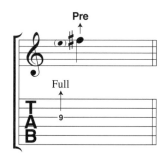

PRE-BEND & RELEASE: Bend the note as indicated. Strike it and release the note back to the original pitch.

UNISON BEND: Strike the two notes simultaneously and bend the lower note up to the pitch of the higher.

BEND & RESTRIKE: Strike the note and bend as indicated then restrike the string where the symbol occurs.

BEND, HOLD AND RELEASE: Same as bend and release but hold the bend for the duration of the tie.

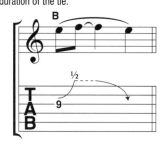

BEND AND TAP: Bend the note as indicated and tap the higher fret while still holding the bend.

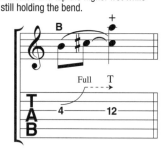

VIBRATO: The string is vibrated by rapidly bending and releasing the note with the fretting hand.

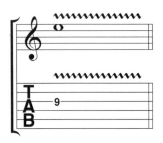

HAMMER-ON: Strike the first (lower) note with one finger, then sound the higher note (on the same string) with another finger by fretting it without picking.

PULL-OFF: Place both fingers on the notes to be sounded, Strike the first note and without picking, pull the finger off to sound the second (lower) note.

LEGATO SLIDE (GLISS): Strike the first note and then slide the same fret-hand finger up or down to the second note. The second note is not struck.

NOTE: The speed of any bend is indicated by the music notation and tempo.

SHIFT SLIDE (GLISS & RESTRIKE): Same as legato slide, except the second note is struck.

TRILL: Very rapidly alternate between the notes indicated by continuously hammering on and pulling off.

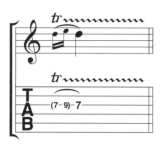

TAPPING: Hammer ("tap") the fret indicated with the pick-hand index or middle finger and pull off to the note fretted by the fret hand.

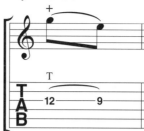

PICK SCRAPE: The edge of the pick is rubbed down (or up) the string, producing a scratchy sound.

MUFFLED STRINGS: A percussive sound is produced by laying the fret hand across the string(s) without depressing, and striking them with the pick hand.

NATURAL HARMONIC: Strike the note while the fret-hand lightly touches the string directly over the fret indicated.

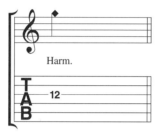

PINCH HARMONIC: The note is fretted normally and a harmonic is produced by adding the edge of the thumb or the tip of the index finger of the pick hand to the normal pick attack.

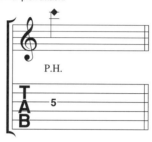

HARP HARMONIC: The note is fretted normally and a harmonic is produced by gently resting the pick hand's index finger directly above the indicated fret (in parentheses) while the pick hand's thumb or pick assists by plucking the appropriate string.

PALM MUTING: The note is partially muted by the pick hand lightly touching the string(s) just before the bridge.

RAKE: Drag the pick across the strings indicated with a single motion.

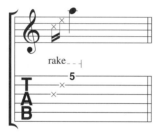

TREMOLO PICKING: The note is picked as rapidly and continuously as possible.

ARPEGGIATE: Play the notes of the chord indicated by quickly rolling them from bottom to top.

SWEEP PICKING: Rhythmic downstroke and/or upstroke motion across the strings.

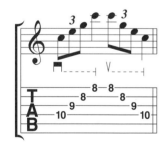

VIBRATO DIVE BAR AND RETURN: The pitch of the note or chord is dropped a specific number of steps (in rhythm) then returned to the original pitch.

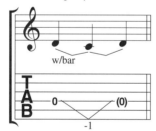

VIBRATO BAR SCOOP: Depress the bar just before striking the note, then quickly release the bar.

VIBRATO BAR DIP: Strike the note and then immediately drop a specific number of steps, then release back to the original pitch.

additional musical definitions

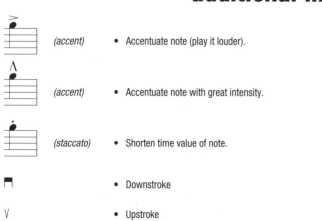

D.S. al Coda — Go back to the sign (%), then play until the bar marked *To Coda* ⊕ then skip to the section marked ⊕ *Coda*.

D.C. al Fine — Go back to the beginning of the song and play until the bar marked *Fine* (end).

tacet — Instrument is silent (drops out).

— Repeat bars between signs.

— When a repeated section has different endings, play the first ending only the first time and the second ending only the second time.

NOTE: Tablature numbers in parentheses mean: 1. The note is sustained, but a new articulation (such as hammer on or slide) begins.
2. A note may be fretted but not necessarily played.

3

down in the tube station at midnight

Words & Music by Paul Weller

© Copyright 1978 Stylist Music Limited/BMG Music Publishing Limited, Bedford House, 69-79 Fulham High Street, London SW6.
This arrangement © Copyright 2000 BMG Music Publishing Limited.
All Rights Reserved. International Copyright Secured.

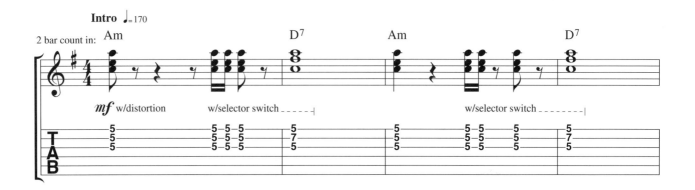

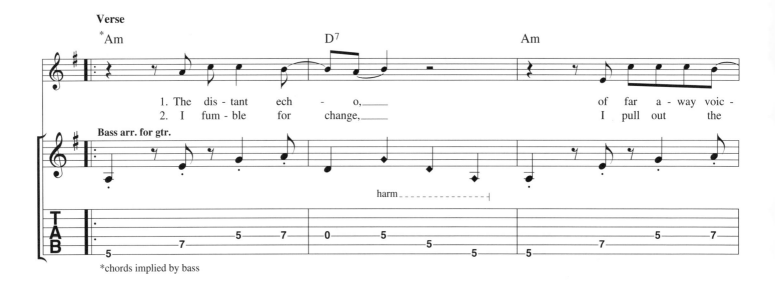

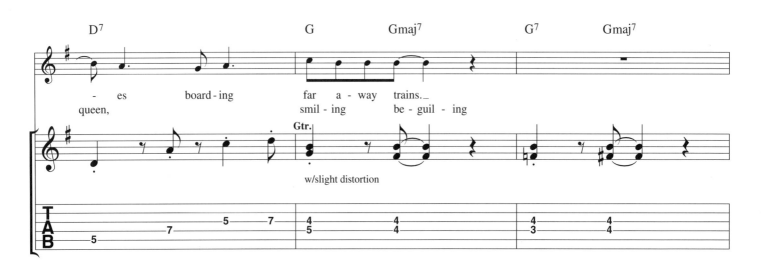

going underground

Words & Music by Paul Weller

© Copyright 1980 Stylist Music Limited/BMG Music Publishing Limited, Bedford House, 69-79 Fulham High Street, London SW6.
This arrangement © Copyright 2000 BMG Music Publishing Limited.
All Rights Reserved. International Copyright Secured.

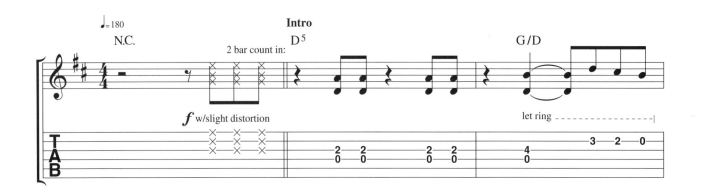

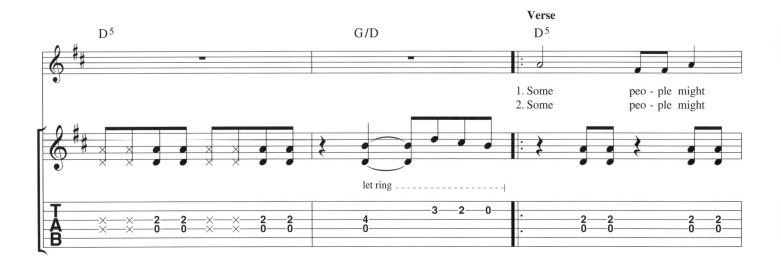

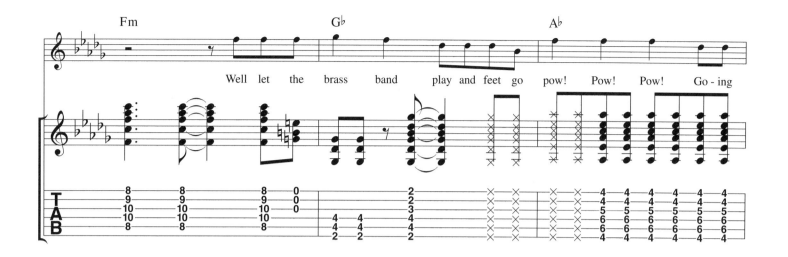
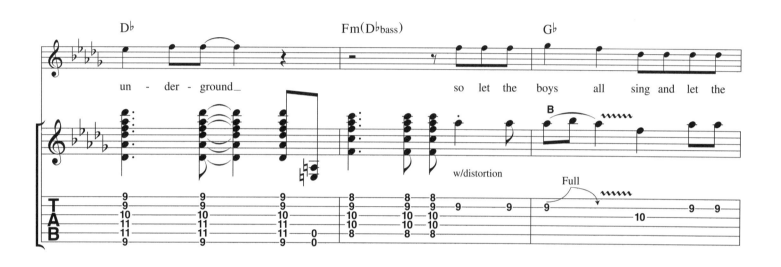
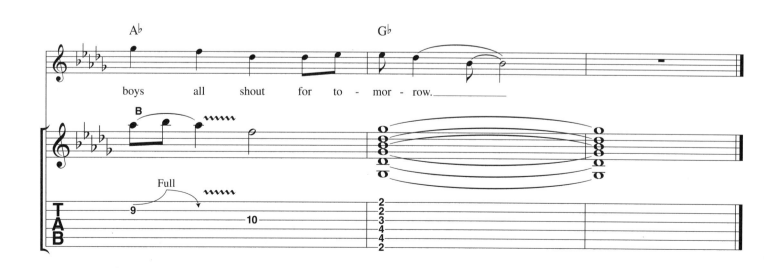

start!

Words & Music by Paul Weller

© Copyright 1980 Stylist Music Limited/BMG Music Publishing Limited, Bedford House, 69-79 Fulham High Street, London SW6.
This arrangement © Copyright 2000 BMG Music Publishing Limited.
All Rights Reserved. International Copyright Secured.

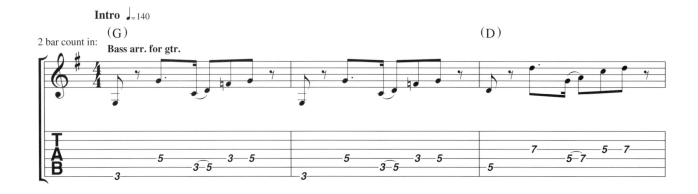

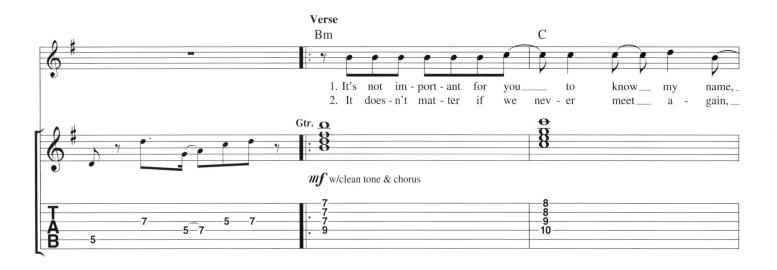

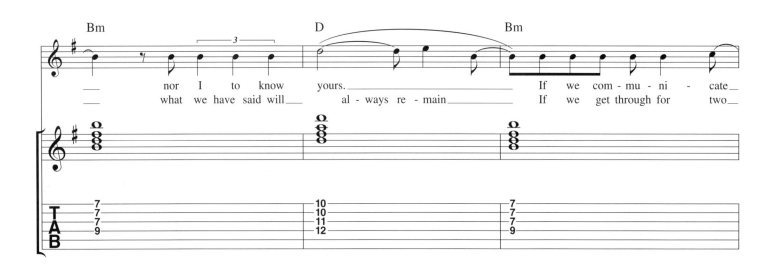

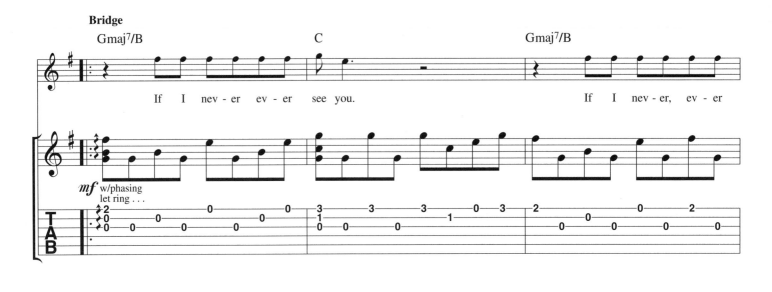
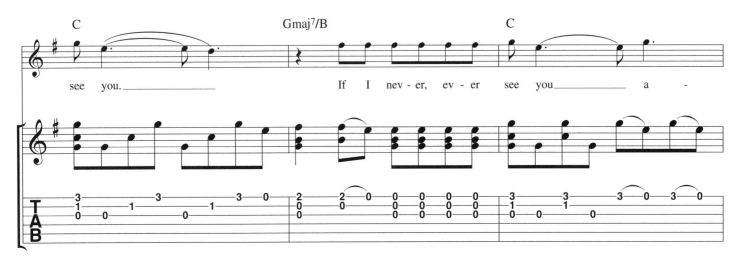
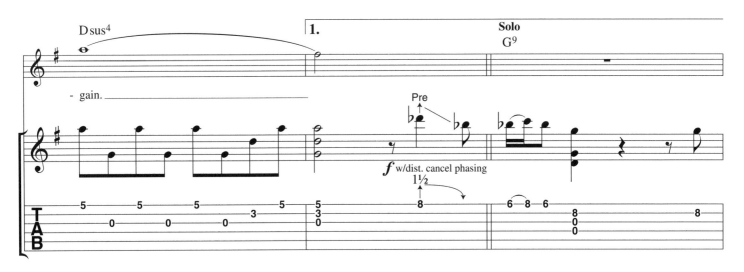

strange town

Words & Music by Paul Weller

© Copyright 1979 Stylist Music Limited/BMG Music Publishing Limited, Bedford House, 69-79 Fulham High Street, London SW6.
This arrangement © Copyright 2000 BMG Music Publishing Limited.
All Rights Reserved. International Copyright Secured.

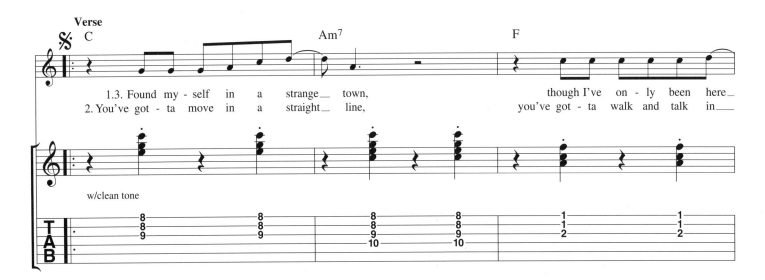

Winner of the Music Industries Association Best Printed Publication 1999

play guitar with...
the biggest names in rock

...eric clapton, jimi hendrix, john squire, kirk hammett, mark knopfler, david gilmour, noel gallagher...
and many more!

over 40 great titles

featuring...
Authentic transcriptions in standard notation and tab

plus...
Full band performances on the CD and separate backing tracks for you to play along with

play guitar with... all these

the music book...
- each book contains half a dozen classic songs presented in standard notation and easy-to-play tab, complete with chord symbols and lyrics.

the CD...
- hear the full-band performances on the accompanying CD (minus lyrics), then...
- take the lead and play along with the separate backing tracks.

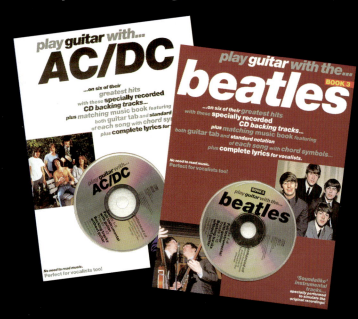

AC/DC
includes:
back in black
highway to hell
whole lotta rosie
Order No. AM955900

the beatles
includes:
day tripper
get back
yesterday
Order No. NO90665

the beatles book 2
includes:
eight days a week
please please me
ticket to ride
Order No. NO90667

the beatles book 3
includes:
here comes the sun
revolution
while my guitar gently weeps
Order No. NO90689

chuck berry
includes:
around and around
johnny b. goode
no particular place to go
Order No. AM943789

black sabbath
includes:
iron man
paranoid
war pigs
Order No. AM955911

blur
includes:
country house
girls and boys
parklife
Order No. AM935320

bon jovi
includes:
livin' on a prayer
wanted dead or alive
you give love a bad name
Order No. AM92558

eric clapton
includes:
layla
sunshine of your love
tears in heaven
Order No. AM950862

phil collins
includes:
another day in paradise
don't lose my number
one more night
Order No. AM928147

the corrs
includes:
forgiven, not forgotten
so young
what can i do
Order No. AM960971

the cranberries
includes:
hollywood
ridiculous thoughts
zombie
Order No. AM941699

dire straits
includes:
money for nothing
romeo and juliet
sultans of swing
Order No. DG70735

david gilmour
includes:
learning to fly
on the turning away
take it back
Order No. AM954602

buddy holly
includes:
rave on
words of love
peggy sue
Order No. AM943734

john lee hooker
includes:
boom boom
the healer
i'm in the mood
Order No. AM951885

b.b. king
includes:
every day I have the blues
rock me baby
the thrill is gone
Order No. AM951874

the kinks
includes:
all day and all of the night
waterloo sunset
you really got me
Order No. AM951863

kula shaker
includes:
govinda
hey dude
hush
Order No. AM943767

john lennon
includes:
cold turkey
happy xmas (war is over)
woman
Order No. AM943756

top bands and artists

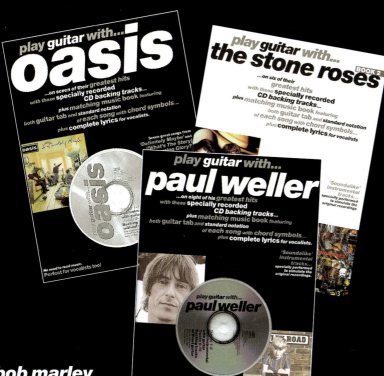

bob marley
includes:
i shot the sheriff
jamming
no woman, no cry
Order No. AM937739

metallica
includes:
enter sandman
fade to black
the unforgiven
Order No. AM92559

metallica book 2
includes:
creeping death
seek and destroy
whiskey in the jar
Order No. AM955977

alanis morissette
includes:
hand in my pocket
ironic
you oughta know
Order No. AM943723

oasis
includes:
cigarettes & alcohol
morning glory
supersonic
Order No. AM935330

ocean colour scene
includes:
the circle
the day we caught the train
the riverboat song
Order No. AM943712

elvis presley
includes:
all shook up
blue suede shoes
hound dog
Order No. AM937090

pulp
includes:
common people
disco 2000
sorted for e's & wizz
Order No. AM938124

the rolling stones
includes:
brown sugar
(i can't get no) satisfaction
jumpin' jack flash
Order No. AM90247

sting
includes:
an englishman in
  new york
fields of gold
if you love somebody
  set them free
Order No. AM928092

the stone roses
includes:
i am the resurrection
i wanna be adored
ten storey love song
Order No. AM943701

the stone roses book 2
includes:
fool's gold
love spreads
one love
Order No. AM955890

suede
includes:
animal nitrate
electricity
we are the pigs
Order No. AM955955

paul weller
includes:
the changingman
out of the sinking
wild wood
Order No. AM937827

the who
includes:
i can see for miles
pinball wizard
substitute
Order No. AM955867

the 60's
includes:
all along the watchtower
  (jimi hendrix)
born to be wild
  (steppenwolf)
not fade away
  (the rolling stones)
Order No. AM957748

the 70's
includes:
all right now (free)
hotel california
  (the eagles)
live and let die (wings)
Order No. AM957759

the 80's
includes:
addicted to love
  (robert palmer)
need you tonight (inxs)
where the streets have
  no name (U2)
Order No. AM957760

the 90's
includes:
everything must go
  (manic street preachers)
love is the law (the seahorses)
wonderwall (oasis)
Order No. AM957770

play guitar with...
sample the whole series with these special compilations...

the gold book
includes eight classic tracks:
jailhouse rock (elvis presley)
johnny b. goode (chuck berry)
layla (eric clapton)
sultans of swing (dire straits)
the healer (john lee hooker)
ticket to ride (the beatles)
woman (john lennon)
you really got me (the kinks)
Order No. AM951907

the platinum book
includes seven great songs:
a design for life
  (manic street preachers)
cigarettes & alcohol (oasis)
disco 2000 (pulp)
elephant stone (stone roses)
govinda (kula shaker)
the changingman (paul weller)
the riverboat song
  (ocean colour scene)
Order No. AM951918

Arthur Dick has transcribed the music and provided the recorded guitar parts for most of the titles in the play guitar with... series, often bringing in other professional specialist musicians to achieve the most authentic sounds possible!

A session guitarist with over twenty years' experience, he has worked with Cliff Richard, Barbara Dickson, Helen Shapiro, Bernie Flint and Chris Rea among others.

Arthur has played in many West End stage shows, and is in regular demand as a session player for TV, radio, and advertising productions.

He currently lectures on jazz and contemporary guitar at University Goldsmith's College, and works as a freelance production consultant.

Available from all good music retailers or, in case of difficulty, contact:

Music Sales Limited
Newmarket Road,
Bury St. Edmunds,
Suffolk IP33 3YB.
telephone 01284 725725
fax 01284 702592

www.musicsales.com

PUB04634

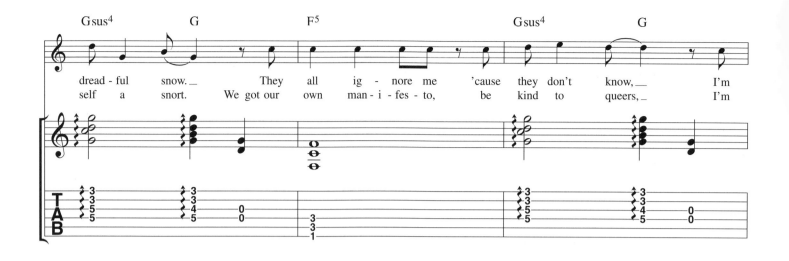
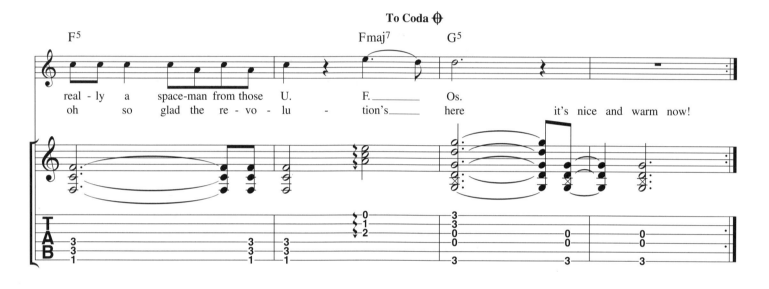
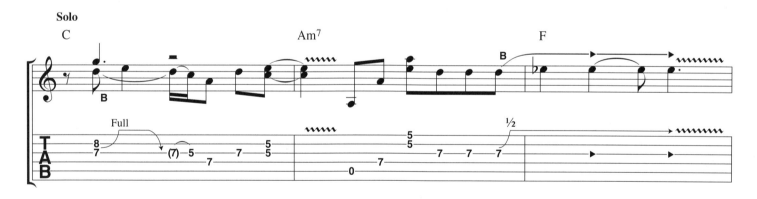
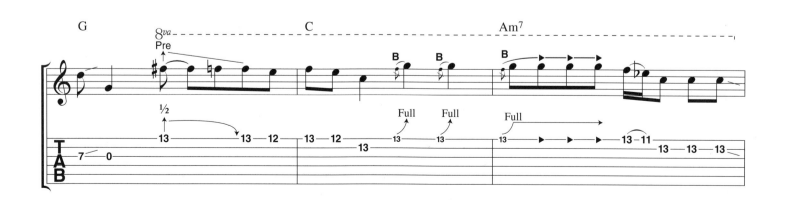

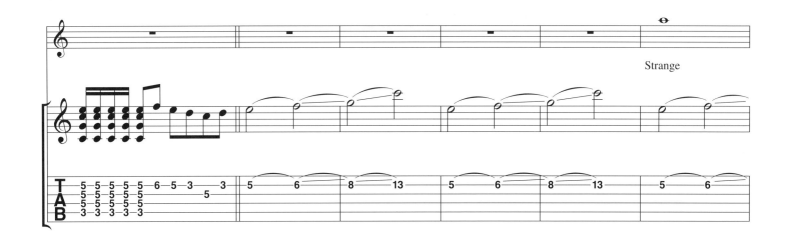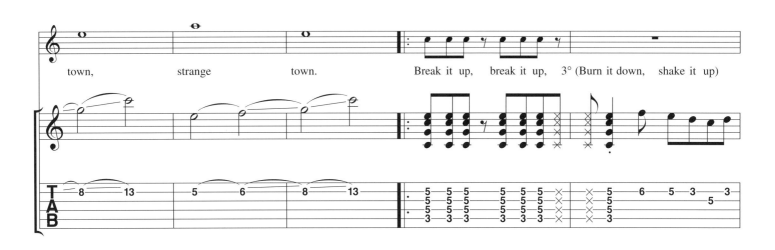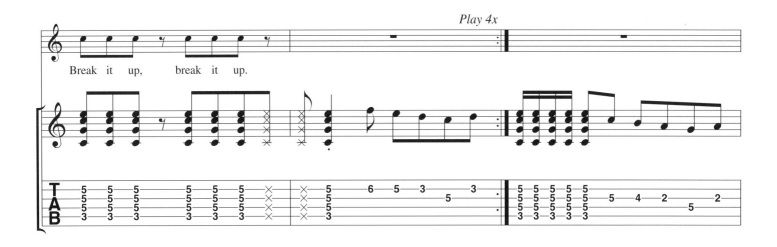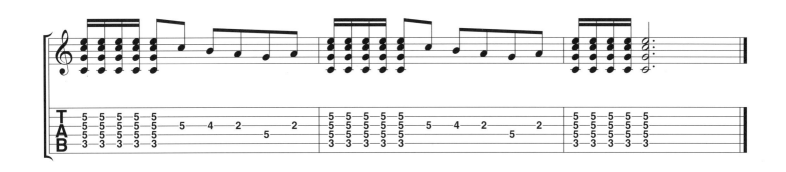

the eton rifles

Words & Music by Paul Weller

© Copyright 1979 Stylist Music Limited/BMG Music Publishing Limited, Bedford House, 69-79 Fulham High Street, London SW6.
This arrangement © Copyright 2000 BMG Music Publishing Limited.
All Rights Reserved. International Copyright Secured.

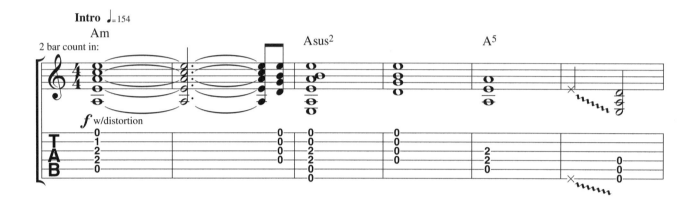

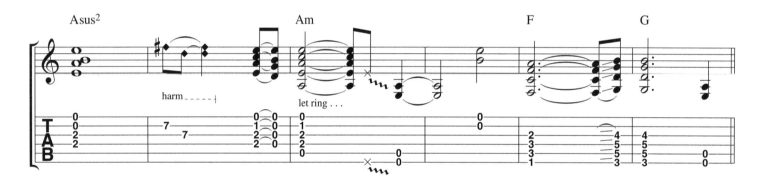

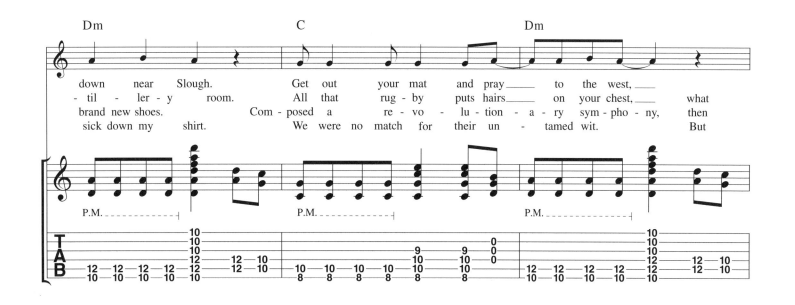
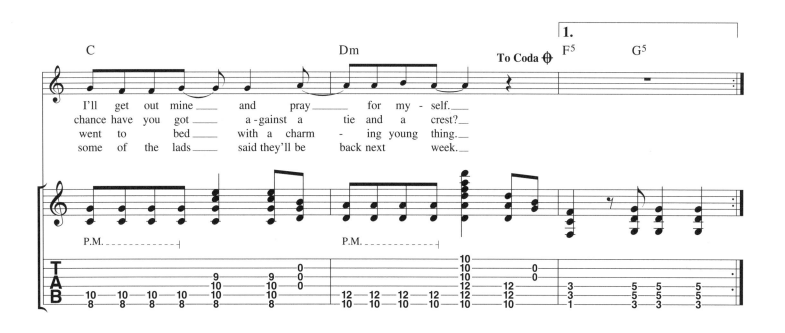
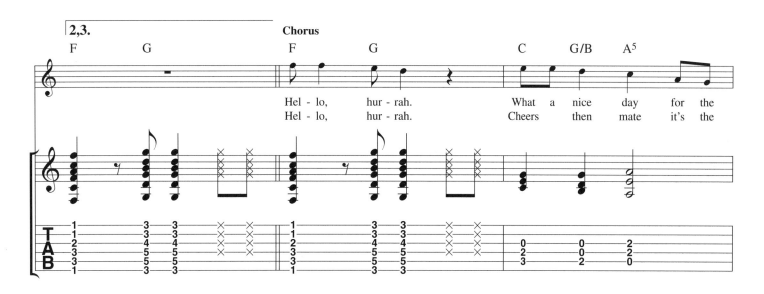

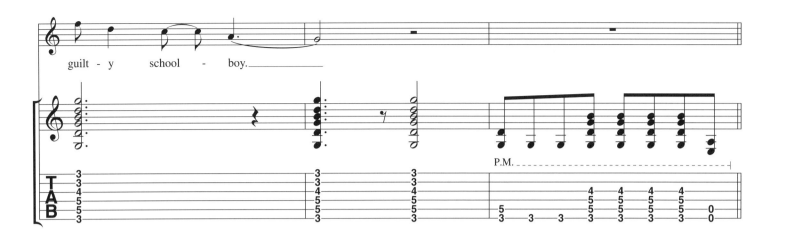
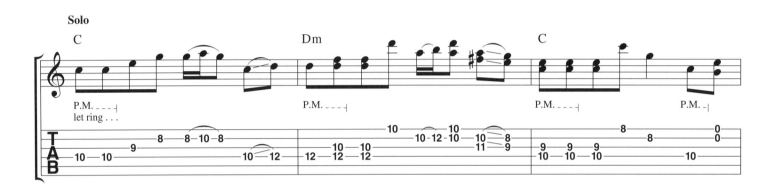
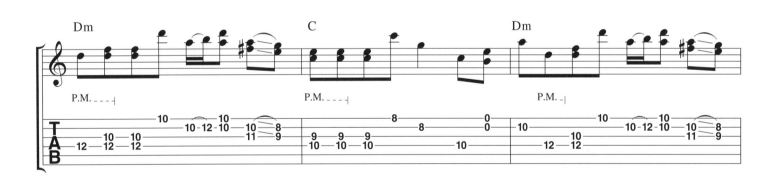
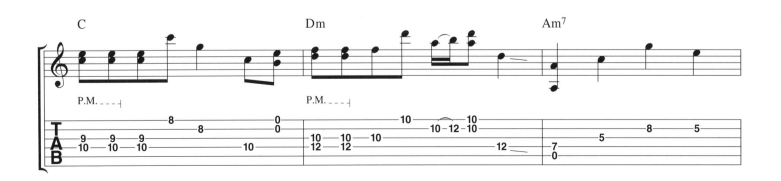

Bridge

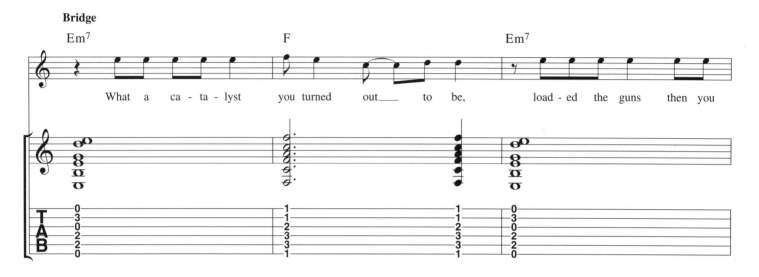

What a ca-ta-lyst you turned out to be, load-ed the guns then you run off home for your tea. Left me stand-ing like a

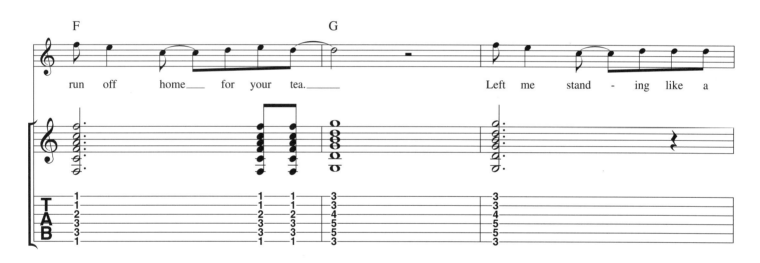

naugh-ty school-boy.

D.S. al Coda

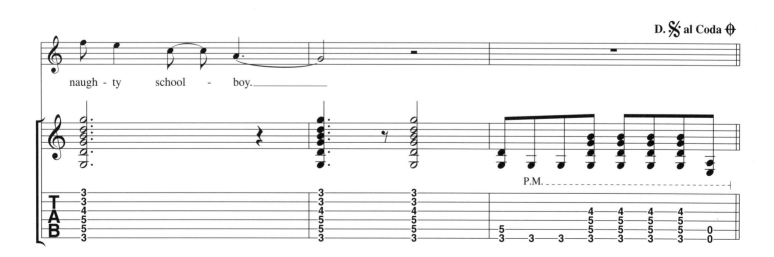

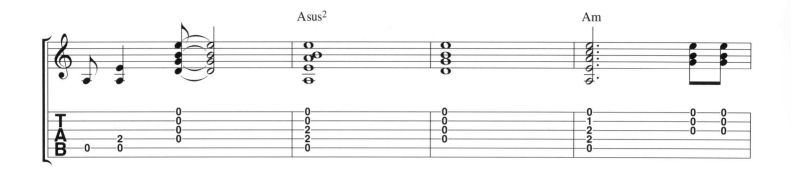
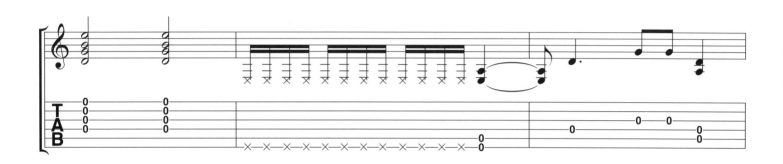
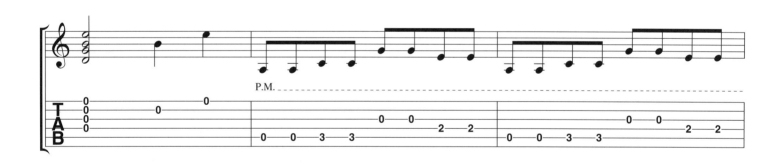
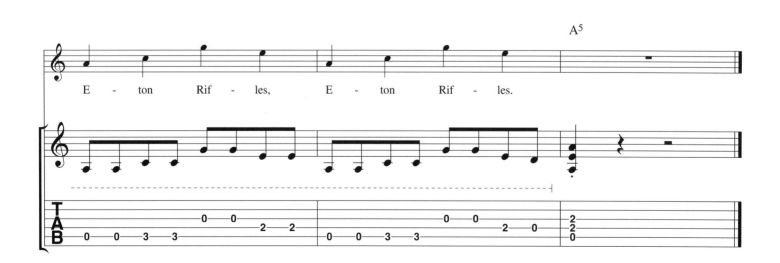

E - ton Rif - les, E - ton Rif - les.

town called malice

Words & Music by Paul Weller

© Copyright 1982 Notting Hill Music (UK) Limited, 8B Berkeley Gardens, London W8.
All Rights Reserved. International Copyright Secured.

37

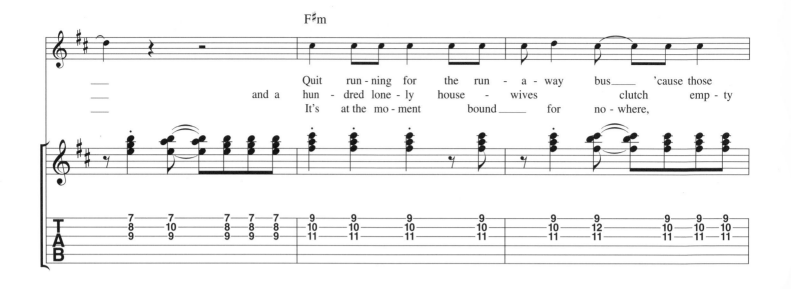

Présentation De La Tablature De Guitare

Il existe trois façons différentes de noter la musique pour guitare : à l'aide d'une portée musicale, de tablatures ou de barres rythmiques.

Les BARRES RYTHMIQUES sont indiquées au-dessus de la portée. Jouez les accords dans le rythme indiqué. Les notes rondes indiquent des notes réelles.

La PORTÉE MUSICALE indique les notes et rythmes et est divisée en mesures. Cette division est représentée par des lignes. Les notes sont : do, ré, mi, fa, sol, la, si.

La PORTÉE EN TABLATURE est une représentation graphique des touches de guitare. Chaque ligne horizontale correspond à une corde et chaque chiffre correspond à une case.

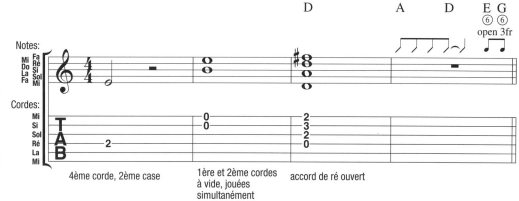

Notation Spéciale De Guitare : Définitions

TIRÉ DEMI-TON : Jouez la note et tirez la corde afin d'élever la note d'un demi-ton (étape à moitié).

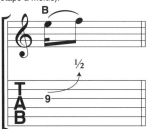

TIRÉ PLEIN : Jouez la note et tirez la corde afin d'élever la note d'un ton entier (étape entière).

TIRÉ D'AGRÉMENT : Jouez la note et tirez la corde comme indiqué. Jouez la première note aussi vite que possible.

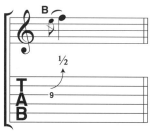

TIRÉ QUART DE TON : Jouez la note et tirez la corde afin d'élever la note d'un quart de ton.

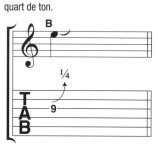

TIRÉ ET LÂCHÉ : Jouez la note et tirez la corde comme indiqué, puis relâchez, afin d'obtenir de nouveau la note de départ.

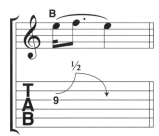

TIRÉ ET REJOUÉ : Jouez la note et tirez la corde comme indiqué puis rejouez la corde où le symbole apparaît.

PRÉ-TIRÉ : Tirez la corde comme indiqué puis jouez cette note.

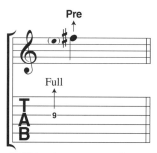

PRÉ-TIRÉ ET LÂCHÉ : Tirez la corde comme indiqué. Jouez la note puis relâchez la corde afin d'obtenir le ton de départ.

HAMMER-ON: Jouez la première note (plus basse) avec un doigt puis jouez la note plus haute sur la même corde avec un autre doigt, sur le manche mais sans vous servir du médiator.

PULL-OFF: Positionnez deux doigts sur les notes à jouer. Jouez la première note et sans vous servir du médiator, dégagez un doigt pour obtenir la deuxième note, plus basse.

GLISSANDO : Jouez la première note puis faites glisser le doigt le long du manche pour obtenir la seconde note qui, elle, n'est pas jouée.

GLISSANDO ET REJOUÉ : Identique au glissando à ceci près que la seconde note est jouée.

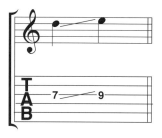

HARMONIQUES NATURELLES : Jouez la note tandis qu'un doigt effleure la corde sur le manche correspondant à la case indiquée.

PICK SCRAPE (SCRATCH) : On fait glisser le médiator le long de la corde, ce qui produit un son éraillé.

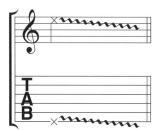

ÉTOUFFÉ DE LA PAUME : La note est partiellement étouffée par la main (celle qui se sert du médiator). Elle effleure la (les) corde(s) juste au-dessus du chevalet.

CORDES ÉTOUFFÉES : Un effet de percussion produit en posant à plat la main sur le manche sans relâcher, puis en jouant les cordes avec le médiator.

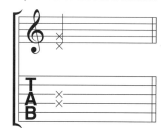

NOTE: La vitesse des tirés est indiquée par la notation musicale et le tempo.

Erläuterung zur Tabulaturschreibweise

Es gibt drei Möglichkeiten, Gitarrenmusik zu notieren: im klassichen Notensystem, in Tabulaturform oder als rhythmische Akzente.

RHYTHMISCHE AKZENTE werden über dem Notensystem notiert. Geschlagene Akkorde werden rhythmisch dargestellt. Ausgeschriebene Noten stellen Einzeltöne dar.

Im **NOTENSYSTEM** werden Tonhöhe und rhythmischer Verlauf festgelegt; es ist durch Taktstriche in Takte unterteilt. Die Töne werden nach den ersten acht Buchstaben des Alphabets benannt.
Beachte: "B" in der anglo-amerkanischen Schreibweise entspricht dem deutschen "H"!

DIE TABULATUR ist die optische Darstellung des Gitarrengriffbrettes. Jeder horizontalen Linie ist eine bestimmte Saite zugeordnet, jede Zahl bezeichnet einen Bund.

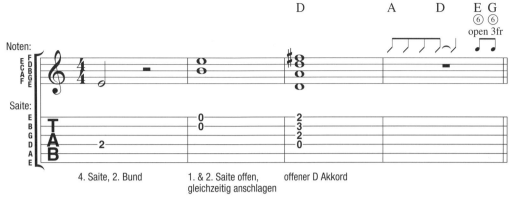

Erklärungen zur speziellen Gitarennotation

HALBTON-ZIEHER: Spiele die Note und ziehe dann um einen Halbton höher (Halbtonschritt).

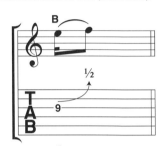

ZIEHEN UND ZURÜCKGLEITEN: Spiele die Note und ziehe wie notiert; lasse den Finger dann in die Ausgangposition zurückgleiten. Dabei wird nur die erste Note angeschlagen.

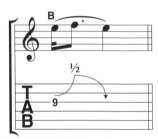

AUFSCHLAGTECHNIK: Schlage die erste (tiefere) Note an; die höhere Note (auf der selben Saite) erklingt durch kräftiges Aufschlagen mit einem anderen Finger der Griffhand.

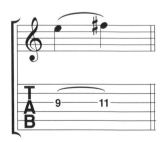

NATÜRLICHES FLAGEOLETT: Berühre die Saite über dem angegebenen Bund leicht mit einem Finger der Griffhand. Schlage die Saite an und lasse sie frei schwingen.

GANZTON-ZIEHER: Spiele die Note und ziehe dann einen Ganzton höher (Ganztonschritt).

ZIEHEN UND NOCHMALIGES ANSCHLAGEN: Spiele die Note und ziehe wie notiert, schlage die Saite neu an, wenn das Symbol "▶" erscheint und lasse den Finger dann zurückgleiten.

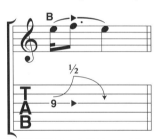

ABZIEHTECHNIK: Setze beide Finger auf die zu spielenden Noten und schlage die erste Note an. Ziehe dann (ohne nochmals anzuschlagen) den oberen Finger der Griffhand seitlich - abwärts ab, um die zweite (tiefere) Note zum klingen zu bringen.

PICK SCRAPE: Fahre mit dem Plektrum nach unten über die Saiten - klappt am besten bei umsponnenen Saiten.

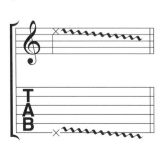

ZIEHER MIT VORSCHLAG: Spiele die Note und ziehe wie notiert. Spiele die erste Note so schnell wie möglich.

ZIEHER VOR DEM ANSCHLAGEN: Ziehe zuerst die Note wie notiert; schlage die Note dann an.

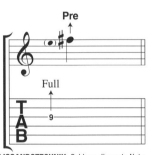

GLISSANDOTECHNIK: Schlage die erste Note an und rutsche dann mit dem selben Finger der Griffhand aufwärts oder abwärts zur zweiten Note. Die zweite Note wird nicht angeschlagen.

DÄMPFEN MIT DER SCHLAGHAND: Lege die Schlaghand oberhalb der Brücke leicht auf die Saite(n).

VIERTELTON-ZIEHER: Spiele die Note und ziehe dann einen Viertelton höher (Vierteltonschritt).

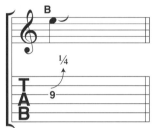

ZIEHER VOR DEM ANSCHLAGEN MIT ZURÜCKGLEITEN: Ziehe die Note wie notiert; schlage die Note dann an und lasse den Finger auf die Ausgangslage zurückgleiten.

GLISSANDOTECHNIK MIT NACHFOLGENDEM ANSCHLAG: Gleiche Technik wie das gebundene Glissando, jedoch wird die zweite Note angeschlagen.

DÄMPFEN MIT DER GRIFFHAND: Du erreichst einen percussiven Sound, indem du die Griffhand leicht über die Saiten legst (ohne diese herunterzudrücken) und dann mit der Schlaghand anschlägst.

AMMERKUNG: Das Tempo der Zieher und Glissandos ist abhängig von der rhythmischen Notation und dem Grundtempo.

Spiegazioni Di Tablatura Per Chitarra

La musica per chitarra può essere annotata in tre diversi modi: sul pentagramma, in tablatura e in taglio ritmico

IL TAGLIO RITMICO è scritto sopra il pentagramma. Percuotere le corde al ritmo indicato. Le teste arrotondate delle note indicano note singole.

IL PENTAGRAMMA MUSICALE mostra toni e ritmo ed è divisa da linee in settori. I toni sono indicati con le prime sette lettere dell'alfabeto.

LA TABLATURA rappresenta graficamente la tastiera della chitarra. Ogni linea orizzontale rappresenta una corda, ed ogni corda rappresenta un tasto.

4° corda, 2° tasto   1° e 2° corda aperte, suonate insieme   accordo D aperto

Definizioni Per Annotazioni Speciali Per Chitarra

SEMI-TONO CURVATO: percuotere la nota e curvare di un semitono (1/2 passo).

TONO CURVATO: Percuotere la nota e curvare di un tono (passo intero).

NOTA BREVE, CURVATA: percuotere la nota e curvare come indicato. Suonare la prima nota il più velocemente possibile.

QUARTO DI TONO, CURVATO: Percuotere la nota e curvare di un quarto di passo.

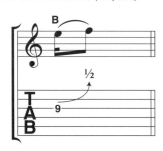 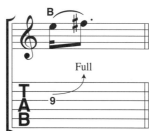 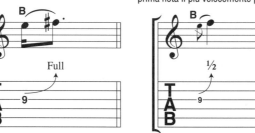 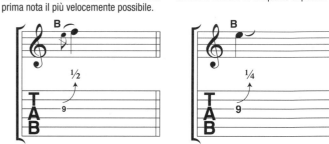

CURVA E LASCIA: Percuotere la nota e curvare come indicato, quindi rilasciare indietro alla nota originale.

CURVA E RIPERCUOTI: Percuotere la nota e curvare come indicato poi ripercuotere la corda nel punto del simbolo.

PRE-CURVA: Curvare la nota come indicato e quindi percuoterla.

PRE-CURVA E RILASCIO: Curvare la nota come indicato. Colpire e rilasciare la nota indietro alla tonalità indicata.

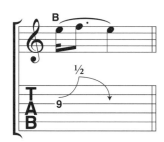 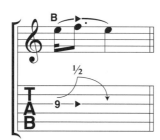  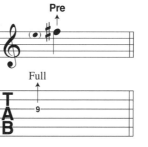

MARTELLO-COLPISCI: Colpire la prima nota (in basso) con un dito; quindi suona la nota più alta (sulla stessa corda) con un altro dito, toccandola senza pizzicare.

TOGLIERE: Posizionare entrambe le dita sulla nota da suonare. Colpire la prima nota e, senza pizzicare, togliere le dita per suonare la seconda nota (più in basso).

LEGATO SCIVOLATO (GLISSATO): Colpire la prima nota e quindi far scivolare lo stesso dito della mano della tastiera su o giù alla seconda nota. La seconda nota non viene colpita.

CAMBIO SCIVOLATO (GLISSARE E RICOLPIRE): Uguale al legato - scivolato eccetto che viene colpita la seconda nota.

  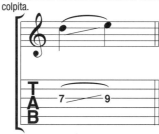 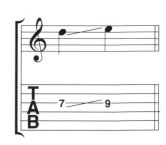

ARMONICA NATURALE: Colpire la nota mentre la mano della tastiera tocca leggermente la corda direttamente sopra il tasto indicato.

PIZZICA E GRAFFIA: Il limite del pizzicato è tirato su (o giù) lungo la corda, producendo un suono graffiante.

SORDINA CON IL PALMO: La nota è parzialmente attenuata dalla mano del pizzicato toccando la corda (le corde) appena prima del ponte.

CORDE SMORZATE: Un suono di percussione viene prodotto appoggiando la mano della tastiera attraverso la corda (le corde) senza premere, e colpendole con la mano del pizzicato.

 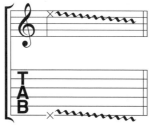 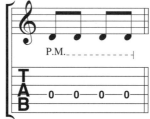 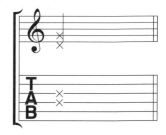

NOTA: La velocità di ogni curvatura è indicata dalle annotazioni musicali e dal tempo.

Tablatura De Guitarra Explicada

La música de guitarra puede ser representada en tres formas diferentes: en un pentagrama, en tablatura, y con acentos rítmicos.

ACENTOS RITMICOS están escritos sobre el pentagrama. Rasguea los acordes cuando te indique los acentos rítmicos. La aparición de una nota rodeada por un círculo indica una sola nota.

El PENTAGRAMA muestra la altura y el ritmo y está dividida en compases mediante unas líneas. La altura de las notas se denominan con las siete primeras notas del alfabeto.

TABLATURA representa gráficamente el diapasón de la guitarra. Cada línea horizontal representa una cuerda, y cada número representa un traste.

Definiciones Especiales Para La Notacion De Guitarra

BEND DE UN SEMITONO : Ataca la nota y eleva la cuerda hasta que esté medio tono por encima de la nota original (1/2 tono).

BEND DE UN TONO : Ataca la nota y eleva de la cuerda hasta que esté un tono por encima de la original (un tono completo).

BEND DE UNA NOTA RAPIDA (GRACE NOTE) : Ataca la nota y eleva la cuerda según se indique en la tablatura. Toca la primera nota tan rápidamente como te sea posible.

BEND DE UN CUARTO DE TONO : Ataca la nota y eleva la cuerda hasta que esté un cuarto de tono (1/4 tono) por encima de la original.

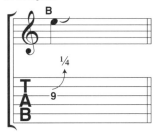

BEND & RELEASE : Ataca la nota y eleva la cuerda según se indica en la tablatura, regresa a la posición y nota iniciales.

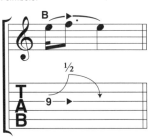

BEND & RESTRIKE : Ataca la nota y eleva la cuerda según lo que indicado entonces ataca de nuevo la cuerda en la que aparece el símbolo.

PRE-BEND : Eleva la cuerda según lo indicado, después atácala.

PRE-BEND & RELEASE : Eleva la cuerda según lo indicado. Atácala y regresa a la posición y nota original.

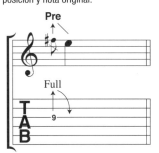

HAMMER-ON : Ataca una nota (grave) con un dedo, entonces haz sonar otra nota más aguda (en la misma cuerda) con otro dedo al tocarla directamente sobre el diapasón, sin atacar la cuerda de nuevo con la púa o los dedos.

PULL-OFF : Sitúa los dedos sobre las notas que desees hacer sonar. Ataca la primera nota y sin utilizar la púa (o los dedos), retira el dedo para hacer que la segunda nota (más grave) suene.

LEGATO SLIDE (GLISS) : Ataca la primera nota y entonces desliza el mismo dedo de la mano situada sobre el diapasón de forma ascendente o descendente hasta alcanzar la segunda nota. La segunda nota no se produce al ser atacada por los dedos o la púa.

SHIFT SLIDE (GLISS & RESTRIKE): Igual que el legato slide, excepto que la segunda nota se ataca con la púa o los dedos.

ARMÓNICOS NATURALES : Ataca la nota mientras que la mano situada sobre el diapasón roza ligeramente la cuerda directamente sobre el traste indicado.

RASPADO DE PÚA : El borde de la púa se desliza de forma descendente (o ascendente) por las cuerdas, provocando un sonido rasposo.

PALM MUTING : La nota es parcialmente apagada al apoyar la mano de la púa ligeramente sobre la cuerdas situándola justo antes del puente.

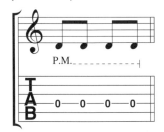

CUERDAS APAGADAS : Un sonido percusivo que se consigue al apoyar la mano situada sobre el diapasón sobre las cuerda (s) relajando la presión sobre éste, mientras que se ataca (n) con la otra mano.

NOTA : La velocidad de cualquier bend está indicada por la notación musical y el tempo.

Music Sales Limited
8-9 Frith Street,
London W1V 5TZ, England.
Music Sales Pty Limited
120 Rothschild Avenue,
Rosebery, NSW 2018, Australia.

Order No. AM963391
ISBN 0-7119-8099-3
This book © Copyright 2000
by Wise Publications

Unauthorised reproduction of any part of this
publication by any means including photocopying
is an infringement of copyright.

Music compiled and arranged by Martin Shellard
Music processed by Andrew Shiels
Cover photographs courtesy of
London Features International

Printed in the United Kingdom by
Caligraving Limited, Thetford, Norfolk.

CD programmed by Martin Shellard
All guitars by Martin Shellard

Your Guarantee of Quality
As publishers, we strive to produce
every book to the highest commercial standards.
The music has been freshly engraved and the book has
been carefully designed to minimise awkward page turns
and to make playing from it a real pleasure.
Particular care has been given to specifying acid-free,
neutral-sized paper made from pulps which have not been
elemental chlorine bleached. This pulp is from farmed
sustainable forests and was produced with
special regard for the environment.
Throughout, the printing and binding have been planned
to ensure a sturdy, attractive publication which
should give years of enjoyment.
If your copy fails to meet our high standards,
please inform us and we will gladly replace it.

www.musicsales.com

Music Sales' complete catalogue describes thousands of titles
and is available in full colour sections by subject, direct from
Music Sales Limited. Please state your areas of interest
and send a cheque/postal order for £1.50 for postage to:
Music Sales Limited, Newmarket Road,
Bury St. Edmunds, Suffolk IP33 3YB.